LIVING LOVE

FROM THE SPIRITUAL HEART

OTHER BOOKS BY JOHN-ROGER

Blessings of Light

The Consciousness of Soul

Divine Essence

Dream Voyages

Forgiveness—
The Key to the Kingdom

Fulfilling Your Spiritual Promise

God Is Your Partner

Inner Worlds of Meditation

The Journey of a Soul

Loving Each Day

Loving Each Day
for Moms & Dads

Loving Each Day for
Peacemakers

Manual on Using the Light

Momentum:
Letting Love Lead
(with Paul Kaye)

Passage Into Spirit

The Path to Mastership

The Power Within You

Psychic Protection

Relationships:
Love, Marriage and Spirit

Sex, Spirit and You

The Spiritual Family

Spiritual High
(with Michael McBay)

The Spiritual Promise

Spiritual Warrior:
The Art of Spiritual Living

The Tao of Spirit

Walking with the Lord

The Way Out Book

Wealth & Higher Consciousness

What's It Like Being You?
(with Paul Kaye)

When Are You Coming Home?
(with Pauli Sanderson)

LIVING LOVE

FROM THE SPIRITUAL HEART

John-Roger, D.S.S.

Mandeville Press
Los Angeles, California

Library of Congress Control Number: 2005938167

Mandeville Press
P.O. Box 513935
Los Angeles, California 90051-1935
323-737-4055
jrbooks@mandevillepress.org
www.mandevillepress.org

Printed in the United States of America
ISBN 1-893020-32-0

CONTENTS

PREFACE

John-Roger is the freest and most loving person I've ever met, and knowing him has been the greatest blessing in my life. So it was a lovely gift for me to compile some of the things he has shared over the years about living love.

J-R, as many call him, founded the Movement of Spiritual Inner Awareness (MSIA) as a physical support for the spiritual work he does, but his work is much greater than any organization. It is Soul Transcendence, assisting people in awakening to the Soul, the divine part in each of us, and then going beyond that into God.

The spiritual consciousness that J-R works through is called the Mystical Traveler, and he has said that "its nature is love, joy, and upliftment. It brings health, wealth, and happiness on the physical level, calm to the emotional level, peace to the mental level, ability to the unconscious level, and the fulfillment of all the dreams to the spiritual level."

This consciousness has always been held, or "anchored," by someone on the planet, and J-R has been doing this since 1963. In 1988, John Morton started being more active as the Mystical Traveler and serves as MSIA's spiritual director. J-R has continued his spiritual work as usual, including participating with MSIA. The Traveler Consciousness is also within each person, J-R teaches, and it is the spiritual energy assisting people in becoming aware of themselves as Soul.

For me, the most important thing about J-R is his steadfast and all-embracing love—for me, for others, for everything. We hope that this book conveys some of the sweetness of that loving and that it touches the loving in you, the loving that is of God.

Betsy Alexander

LIVING LOVE

FROM THE SPIRITUAL HEART

SPIRITUAL LOVE

Love is the essence of all creation, the "glue" that holds everything in its place in relation to all other parts and that allows it all to function. Everything is a manifestation of love, and *loving* is about the closest term I've come up with for the energy of Spirit.

Loving is a process that happens inside you through the grace of Spirit and by your own ability to be in touch with the God within. The loving that you have for yourself and for one another is God's love. There isn't any other love. Your loving heart is God's loving heart. Your body is God's body. The God that you are is all the other "Gods." In God, you have your living and breathing, your coming in and going out, your death and your resurrection. The whole spectrum of your life takes place within God, and anyone who is residing in the power of love is never destroyed, never separated, always free, always up, always growing.

Living love is not just loving from some place deep within you, but living love with every breath. When you breathe in, love breathes in. And when you breathe out, love breathes out. Living love also means that your love extends unconditionally to all things. You love everything present, no exceptions. Living love doesn't care whether you're black or white, female or male, drunk or sober, this or that. It is the expression of the loving heart, which knows no limitations, conditions, or restrictions. It just is—equally.

All love is within you. It's part of infinite supply; in fact, it *is* the infinite supply. It's important for you to keep calling forward the essence of spiritual love every day so you keep lifting higher. Let nothing stop you from this endeavor, for it is more important than any other activity.

Don't look for God and Spirit outside yourself; just awaken to the presence inside. Know that God reigns personally inside you as you, and the Beloved is present. When you look to the Beloved, you separate and create two where there is only one. We are one in God's loving heart, and there is truly only one Beloved: the God-form. You are part of it. Everyone is.

When you are living from the truth of your beingness, you become very realistic about what is. You are able to perceive and work with what is—without having to make any value judgment at all in your mind and emotions. That will be a great freedom to you. You will become able to perceive more and more clearly and with less and less judgment. You will see things for what they are and work from that level. It's a good place to be. That's the way to find God.

The very first Soul Awareness Discourse says that MSIA teaches the brotherhood of man and the Fatherhood of God. Love is the bond that creates the brotherhood, and love will set you free to discover the Fatherhood of God. MSIA teaches the awakening in love. Other groups may teach awakening through anguish, pain, self-denial, abnegation, or fear. We don't teach that. There would be little joy in that path, and the presence of joy is one of the best indicators that the Spirit is present—joy and love.

You can't create love, nor can you create joy. These are expressions of the Soul. Even in the midst of aches and pains, emotional anguish, and negative thinking, there can be joy and love because those are of the Soul. The Soul's first name is Love, its middle name is Truth, and its last name is Everlasting. Love and Truth Everlasting.

The Soul is everywhere. It's in the laughter. It's in the twinkle in the eyes. It's in the touch. It's in the empathy you experience when someone else is hurting. It's in the joy you experience when someone you love is happy. It's in all of that and more.

When something makes you joyfully happy, even though you can't see, touch, feel, hear, or smell it, you're tapping into Spirit. When you feel the joy and goodness bubbling up inside of you for no apparent reason, you're in Spirit. When you feel like laughing and nothing is particularly funny, but the laughter is just an overflow of the good feeling inside, you are in Spirit. It's the peace that goes beyond understanding and the love that stays present no matter what other people do.

Joy is inherent through the Soul. When you have joy—when this happiness just comes up inside of you—then no matter what you do or say or become out there, this center of calm and happiness is not disturbed because it is what it is. Therein is your fulfillment for being on this physical level.

You do experience the Soul directly—not by reflection or interpretation, but directly. You get glimpses of what *is*. You get glimpses of knowing. Loving encompasses and fills everything. Joy shines inwardly. The trials of the world fade in power. All becomes one. You know your Source and your comings and your goings from that Source. All needs are already fulfilled, and there is nothing except loving communion with God. Divine communion is really just *loving*. It's that quality where you experience yourself dancing in your own heart.

So reach into the happiness and joy inside. God is inside, eternal life is inside, the Soul that you are is inside. The Soul is your connection to God's loving heart. The Soul is living water to quench your thirst. The Soul is living food to nourish you. The Soul is the living breath that gives you life. Happiness is inherent in the consciousness of Soul and can only be realized by traveling the inner path.

THE INNER PATH

Spirit is not a process of the outer world. Spirit lives in the inner consciousness. Its voice rings in the silence of your heart. Its movement is in the perfect stillness within. Its greatest expression is in the peace and loving that reside at the core of your beingness.

A lot of people look at their lives and say, "There has to be something better, something more than this." There *is* a lot more than this, but not necessarily on the physical level. Wherever you are, no matter what you are doing or what you have with you, you can have the greatest experience possible: the awareness that you are a child of God and are divine. So begin your inner journey *now*. You will be filled with joy and the glorious feeling of love and caring.

The experience the Mystical Traveler brings to you has to do with Spirit, with God, with pure love that transcends all lower levels and that lifts you into Soul—and then beyond. This experience is Soul Transcendence, to live here and discover the higher reality, to extend into that greater consciousness of Light, of love, of Sound—to be that. Soul Transcendence is the only method that will set you free, and it is your heritage.

That one that is the Traveler shares himself with those who are his Beloveds, those who are the initiates. The Traveler does not offer just an association; the Traveler offers a relationship that abides in the heart, nowhere else. It is a relationship of living love.

The Mystical Traveler speaks through the heart. It speaks loving. It is love, and it will lift you in love. The Traveler's work is love made manifest. When you follow the Traveler, you walk right into his heart, and as you allow it, he walks right into your heart, too.

In that loving place, you are one. It's really nice to awaken to the Traveler Consciousness and the awareness of the Traveler's presence inside you. The Traveler is there waiting. The first time you asked for the Traveler's help—with your eyes, your mind, or your heart—you awakened in his heart.

Now, awaken to the Lord living in and through you. Recognize that your love is God's love and your joy is God's joy and that all you have to do is share—from one God to another. As you continually express love, you will find that you live more and more within the grace of the Traveler, within his higher love and within his eternal blessings. It is the realization of this that can lift you into that spiritual form that is the answer, that is the remedy, that is the solution to all dilemmas. Place your love in the heart of the Traveler. That is living love. Everything, even your breathing, becomes loving. Your touch becomes loving. Your whole approach becomes loving. Then everything you do, you do for love.

So embrace the Traveler in your inner awareness. Know that form as the essence of yourself, your Inner Master, which is closer to you than your breath, more real than any other level. Know that in the Traveler's love, you will walk straight into the heart of God and awaken to the pure form of God's beingness within you.

The Traveler comes in on love, so move to love and you'll find the Traveler entirely present in your heart. You'll feel the Traveler behind your eyes, sharing your world with you. You'll sense the Traveler walking beside you, touching your hand, as you walk down the street. As you move to that quiet place inside, you'll feel the Traveler's embrace and know that you and the Traveler are one. And the next big step is for your loving to come forward so you recognize the Traveler as you.

The Traveler's love is with you, and his heart awaits your greater awakening. The Traveler is always with you. All you need do is attune yourself to the loving you share and follow as the Traveler leads you home to the heart of God.

REACHING INTO SPIRIT

You reach into Spirit by building the strength of Spirit through spiritual exercises. And the only way you can have the experience, the transcendental knowledge, is to have a spiritual transport that can move you from this physical level into the spiritual realms. This spiritual transport has three parts: the first is love, the second is devotion, and the third is the Mystical Traveler. You travel by way of the Sound Current, the supreme energy force, which is also known as the Holy Spirit, the Unstruck Melodies of Spirit, or God's Unspoken Voice. You ride the Sound Current back through the formlessness into the heart of God.

When you're doing spiritual exercises, you hear the Sound and follow it, but if you don't also have the Light, you may stumble and fall. So you bring in the

Light to see better. You also need love because that is the motivation to keep going. So you need the Light and Sound and love.

Spiritual exercises are a manifestation of loving, your loving of Spirit and God, and God's loving of you. When you chant your initiation tone, you are singing the song of loving that has been sung by the saints and sages of all time. It's a joyful process. Doing spiritual exercises can also bring you the same experiences as those of a mystic; chanting your initiation tone can bring you the realizations that will rip the veil between this mundane world and the experience of the heart of God.

As you chant the names of God, as you live from a loving place, and as you maintain those practices no matter what, you find that the Beloved starts appearing inside of you, as you. You find yourself becoming the Promised One. The Beloved lives for you, in you, as you. It's not designed for this world. As you live within that spiritual form, you may find that the world shifts for you, but it will be more through your perception of it and participation in it rather than from anything outside yourself.

When you are devoted to the Sound and the Light, you are devoted to that consciousness which is the Traveler, you are devoted to yourself, and you are devoted to each other. And when you are working with the Traveler, all things unfold in their right and proper timing. You can assist by loving yourself every step of the way, by doing your spiritual exercises to gain a greater perspective on what you are experiencing, by loving the people around you and treating them with kindness, and by living with integrity and honesty.

When you live in the love of the Traveler, it is not necessary to sacrifice the mind, give up the desires, or eliminate the self, because that has already been done. It is over, and now you need only live joyfully and in harmony with your true nature. You can become the spiritual one for whom you have been waiting. All that has been promised to you is here and now. Some people are waiting for a good time sometime in the future, but it can be right here, right now. The good time is present, here and now, because the love is present.

What matters, in each and every moment, is that you are loving. Be loving to yourself and to others. When you are doing that in the reality of each moment, all dilemmas will fall into line, and you will begin attuning yourself to the greater love that is the love of the Traveler. The first step is to be loving.

My love is always with you. Use it to lift and sustain yourself until you know your own divinity.

THE NEVER-ENDING JOURNEY

When you do your spiritual exercises, you practice going in and out of the body. You practice traversing the spiritual realms beyond the physical level. Death is nothing more than transiting from this level to another level, and you can become quite adept at that. Sometimes you do it unconsciously, and other times you do it with some degree of conscious awareness. There is value in learning to travel consciously because it gives you a sense of confidence and reduces fear. When the time comes for your physical death, it will be just one more lifting out of your body, except that you won't be coming back.

When you place the name of God in every situation and every moment, then in the moment death overtakes you, you'll remember the name of the

Lord as a matter of habit, and you won't be caught in death's throes. Or at the moment of death, if the Lord calls your spiritual name, you'll be so attuned to listening inwardly that you'll hear it, respond, and move immediately into God. You'll defeat death and rise into greater life. Either way, you'll demonstrate the ability to go immediately into the line of transcendental energy that overcomes death.

Some people are afraid to die because they don't know what the next step will be. It's loving. When you die, you go straight to loving. So live *now* into that part that will live—the love, the humbleness, and the truth that is eternally present. Then life blooms forth and is enhanced by the Lord's name, by calling on the sweetness of God's salvation.

You might feel good about yourself if you could realize that you were established in Soul consciousness and that while you were living in Soul consciousness, you could watch your body evolve itself through its final process and release itself from the wheel of incarnation. You could then reside in the majesty and glory of who you really are.

The Traveler teaches longevity to clear as much karma as possible. And if you live every day of your life in the most efficient, dynamic, and uplifting way possible, then when it comes time to leave this field of reality for the greater spiritual reality, it can be completed with grace and ease. It will be a joyful completion, graduation, and new beginning.

LIVING IN LOVING

God's name is living love, and these are the actions of love: increase your Light, continue your development, be a joy to everyone you see, lift yourself continually. Do everything with your attention on getting a smile on your face and love in your eyes. Look at everything through love. Do everything in God's name, and you will be walking straight towards God.

When you bring yourself into a loving consciousness with all things and with the one consciousness that is everywhere, peace and harmony will enfold your heart and you will recognize within every level of your beingness that there is only love. Let love be your guide, your breath, your life. Then you live in the heart of God and are renewed every moment through His love.

When you come to those peak experiences wherein you find love residing, identify them, internalize them, and make them glow so you can find them again when you start to go off your path. Go into those loving places often, and build that strong place within where you can say, "My Father and I are one."

Life is awareness, awareness is life, and the degree of your awareness is the degree of your loving. The greater your awareness, the greater your loving; the more you open to Spirit, the more clearly you see and the more completely you love. When you become one with Spirit, there is no separation from anything or anyone.

The Traveler doesn't ask a lot of you. He asks you to do your spiritual exercises every day, to love one another, and to live without hurting yourself or others, in ways that will nurture and care for yourself and others. Within those parameters, all the choices are yours.

So take the time to really foster your love for yourself. Do spiritual exercises so you can lift above the mundane activities of your life and see how you are working things out and learning the lessons that are important to you. Then you can love yourself even though you have made mistakes along the way.

And do yourself a favor. Live honestly, with integrity, with loving kindness and charity for your fellow beings. Your reward will be your ability to do better and the awakening of Spirit inside you to higher levels of expression. If the key is to be loving, you'll give up every consideration, every hesitation, and every reason not to be loving, and you'll be loving in every situation in your life.

You will be happy when you learn to center yourself in your own divine love, love that flows out to all God's creatures. So stand up in the beingness of your own love, and let that love be your connection to all things. When you can enter your loving, your spiritual center, it doesn't much matter what the world presents to you. You have the inner resources to create your own happiness and fulfillment.

While you are here, my wish is for you to be loving, to serve God and your fellow men, and to be open to all the blessings that are already yours. And don't forget that this world is not your home. Your home lies beyond the Soul realm, and you get there through Soul Transcendence. Your job here is to experience. That's all you have to do. It is in the *loving* of your experience, the *loving* of your expression, that you discover the inner joy, the bliss that is your indication of the presence of the Traveler. So let's live in the spirit of Light and love and happiness and joy, and let's find God within and let's find God without.

TAKING CARE OF YOURSELF

Living love is loving yourself first, so that you can love others. It's taking care of yourself, so that you can help take care of others. It's doing those things that are good for you, so that you'll be happy, healthy, and a joy to be with. Love is everywhere when there is loving in you.

To be healthy physically, be healthy in your emotions, your actions, your mind, your thoughts, your heart. Speak kind words to yourself and to others. Do those things that will support your body physically. Reach out and touch others. Take responsibility for your actions, and handle your responsibilities in an appropriate manner.

There is nothing wrong with being selfish. Eating and getting proper rest are selfish for the body, thinking nice thoughts is selfish for the mind, feeling good is selfish for the emotions, and doing spiritual exercises to rouse the Soul that may be sleeping is selfish for the Spirit. Those are all healthy activities. If other people fit in with your plan for taking care of yourself, that can be fantastic. If they undermine the plan, let them go their own way. Let them go in love, with good thoughts and good feelings towards them—but let them go if they do not support you in those things that are good for you. Experience the devotion to yourself that allows you to take care of yourself.

Going to a doctor is a form of love. It's a way of saying that you are starting to take better care of yourself, and taking care of yourself is loving yourself. You release the downward flow of energy and circulate it back up again.

This physical body is truly a temple of the Spirit, for the Spirit resides in each one of us. And you can build your body so that it does not become a heavy body, but a light body, so the Spirit can work more closely with you. When you reach a harmony within you, you can take cells that have been out of balance and place a ring of love around them and hold them in balance for five, ten, fifteen years. Love and joy and happiness can change the frequency of cell structure from the "doom and gloom" of a cell disintegrating to a lilting, joyful quality of a cell lifting into balance and harmony.

Take care of yourself on all levels. Do those things that will be uplifting. Be with other people who are following the upward path. Be loving to yourself and to others. Chant the sacred names of God. Open your heart to God's presence and walk joyfully in His loving embrace.

LOVING IT ALL

The key to breaking free is to love yourself and to love each experience that comes to you whether it appears to be negative or positive. Love it all equally. Love it all, own it all—and you will be free.

Enough love will handle all things. If you are having difficulty handling something, you don't have enough love for that thing. So your next step is laid out right in front of you: get some more love. If there are still areas of your life that cause you difficulty, bless them. Indeed, those areas *are* your blessings because they move you to seek the Kingdom of God. If all things were perfect here, you might forget all about your spiritual direction.

When you can look at your life in perspective, you will see the humor of it. Enjoy it. Enjoy yourself in all your escapades. When you do, it's easy for the loving to come present and manifest itself in everything you do. So love your depression, love your despair, love your anger, love your confusion, love your upset. Love is the key—total, unconditional love. Even when you don't feel like loving, you love the feeling of not feeling like loving.

When things are going badly, sit down and say, "I love me anyway." Keep chanting your tone, keep loving yourself, and keep on keeping on. Even your negative experiences are gifts from Spirit to build your strength, your awareness, your empathy, and your loving, so thank God for them. When you are secure in your knowledge of God's love for you, you know that *everything* that happens is to lift you and move you closer to your own divinity. I found out a long time ago that what the Lord does is perfect, and there is nothing designed to hurt or harm you.

Love your karma, also. It is your opportunity to learn and to gain wisdom. By loving even your negative creations, you can shift their energy and release karma. You have the opportunity to change the karmic flow of your life through your ability to be loving. By loving the God in yourself and others, you can move into a path of greater unfoldment. Instead of looking at the factors of your life and saying, "That's my karma, so I can't help it," you might say, "That's my karma, and I will fulfill it so I am free." Through loving, you can complete your karma.

The Traveler is working to show you how to live a life of honesty and integrity and to be a responsible creator. He won't do it for you or take those lessons from you, but he loves you through anything you create. He's with you and supports you as you build your own inner support system and keep it activated so that you have the strength to travel the upward path and reach Soul consciousness. The Traveler goes through it all with you because he loves you. All you have to do is turn towards the Traveler. He is always with you, and you'll always find him as soon as you look inside.

You are blessed and you are loved because you are divine. You never walk one step of your life path alone, for the Light of God is always with you.

GOD IN FRONT OF YOU

It can be a beautiful, beautiful world when you realize that the divine essence that is *you* is also within everyone else. When you are attuned to the Soul that you are, you see the Soul in everyone. No matter where you look, no matter what you see, it is a manifestation of divine love. That which you see is God standing in front of you. God may be many different sizes, shapes, and forms, but it is all God, all divine love made manifest.

And truly, nothing on this planet is more important than people, than the Soul that is each person. As you learn to recognize the Soul, the divinity in each person, you will be able to love all that you meet. So treat people as they deserve to be treated, as the extension of God that they are, and look for the divine in all things and in everyone.

Letting divine love flow through you is very easy. All you do is move to a neutral position, not one of belief or disbelief, not one of judgment or prejudice, but one of receptiveness. As soon as you judge, as soon as you take someone else's inventory, you strike against divine love. Loving is a very neutral state. It's "I love you if you're good, I love you if you're bad, I love you if you're not doing either one of those."

On this level, you can best serve your own spiritual progression by expressing lovingly towards everyone you encounter. So as you go about your daily life, be kind and friendly to others. Kindness is authentic, heartfelt action towards somebody, being friendly is being loving, and the love we teach in MSIA is the love of understanding, acceptance, and support. It's the love that says, "Whatever you do is fine. I'll assist you, and I'll lift you." It's a peaceful, easy-going, flowing love. And a statement of your maturing behavior is to love just because you're going to love: "I love because of who *I* am."

There is nothing quite as nice as sharing your loving heart. A little loving can awaken others to their own Light, and then they, in turn, can share it with more people. We can change the world this way. You can be in a state of constant prayer for the upliftment of everyone, full of love for the essence of each one's beingness. Then, wherever you go, people will thank God that you're there.

So take good care of yourself. Hold good feelings and thoughts in your mind so you can share that goodness with other people. When they are down, help lift them by just being you. When you use this approach as a method, it becomes a way of life. If you did that from now on, you could help to create a wind that would clean the planet.

LOVING COMMUNICATION

Love is the only channel for clear communication, and the quality of loving communicates far more than words. That's important to keep in mind as you deal with people. What will truly communicate Spirit and God to others is your loving. The words won't matter much. You can say, "Where's a good place to eat?" or "What's new with you?" or "Have you read any good books lately?"—and if you ask with a consciousness of loving support, people will get the loving behind the words.

Follow the direction of Spirit, which will be towards honest and open communication, brought forward with great love and great gentleness. People are much too valuable and much too precious to hurt or abuse or offend in any way at all. Always speak kind words and speak from loving.

Honesty can be a great expression of loving. When you share with a person in *loving* honesty, you do not hurt or push away the person. You assist the person to a new level inside himself or herself. Remember that "being honest" is not license to jam your opinion at someone or to hurt them in the name of "truth." Always be loving in your approach. And if you feel like you'd like to give someone a piece of your mind, give them, instead, a piece of your heart. Give them love.

If your spouse, a loved one, or a friend has the courage to be honest with you, let them know you appreciate it and give them loving support so they have the freedom to be more of who they are with you. It will be tremendously rewarding for you and others if you become a good listener. Let people talk to you. Love them and let them know you care. You don't have to offer any solutions; they'll come up with their own if you let them. All you have to do is lovingly be there with them.

If you are sharing with people and you are one step ahead of them in working out your karmic patterns, be careful that you don't block them with your enthusiasm to serve by telling them how to do it. Sometimes you have to sit back, put your hand over your mouth, and let others talk and talk and talk.

Listening is one of the deepest, most profound signs of loving—listening to yourself and listening to others. Your heart goes out and wraps around them, and God's spirit of loving embraces you both.

YOUR ONENESS WITH OTHERS

When you are attuned to Spirit and are experiencing the love of Spirit, the negativity of others does not matter. There is love and forgiveness for everything and everyone. So sacrifice your anger for your loving expression. Sacrifice your self-righteousness (which is "wrongeousness") for kindness and loving words. Sacrifice your point of view for the highest good. Then you are living the Christ Consciousness and living in grace.

We are all one. So when you cannot accept and love one person, you create separation towards everyone. You create a separation between you and your God, between you and the God in everyone. A way to move from separation into grace is to throw away your swords of righteousness, throw away your judgments and your sense that you know what is best for other people, allow others (and yourself) to make mistakes in this world, and love them (and yourself) anyway.

Truth and love are cohesive. They erase separation and bring balance. When you start worrying about others and what they are going to do with their lives, you are in a process of separation. You have either separated yourself from them by judging what they are doing, or you have separated them from their own process of unfoldment by your concern that they have somehow gone astray. Let it go. Let the truth manifest in them however they are aligned with it. It doesn't have to be your way.

If there is anybody in this world that you have any type of feeling towards other than a good feeling, get it out of you. Work on it like you've never worked on anything before—because you cannot see the face of God unless you can turn towards God, and you cannot turn towards God if you are blocked in an area every time you think of it. To see the face of God, you have to see the face of God in all people. And that takes a lot of courage because you have to continually move yourself past your personality, prejudices, and points of view until you recognize your oneness with those other personalities out there.

Maybe you watch a colleague at work make an error and think, "Idiot!" You may not even say it out loud and may hardly acknowledge it to yourself because it flashes through your consciousness so quickly. And that may be the very subtle level of judgment that blocks your love and keeps you stuck.

When you're irritated with somebody, start to love the irritation because you might not be able to love the person just yet, but you can start to love the irritation. You start to mix it with the ingredients of Spirit. Remember, too, that you can love everyone, but you can be very selective about those with whom you will share closely. And if you can't love certain people, be neutral towards them. Don't hate them. Just let them go.

If some people continually evoke a negative response within you, you can put these people in the Light, knowing full well that they are not responsible for your negative response; *you* are responsible for it. Things then become so much easier because you cannot hate anyone or push them away. You can't hate them because they are helping you to balance your past actions, to become clearer, and to lift your consciousness.

Let yourself know the closeness and the fellowship of the Beloved within you, and know that the apparent differences you perceive on the outer are only different reflections of the same inner essence. No matter what anyone says or does, you can look at that person *inside* of you and feel loving for them and find upliftment. And if you want to see people perfectly, look at them through the eyes of love. When you do, strange as it may seem, everybody has a loving consciousness.

Do you love and assist those you are with? Do you keep in mind that all people are doing the best they can?

Do you use the Light in all situations to assist and uplift? If that's your expression, you are moving into Soul.

LOVING SERVICE

Love becomes a living thing when it is shared with others; at that point, *love* becomes *loving*. As you choose a path of loving service, you are aligning yourself with Spirit, and there is a great field of loving that moves through the people who are united in the Traveler's love. It's manifested through each one of you as you are helping, caring, working, being, and loving with one another.

Loving is the most important quality you can nurture in yourself. In the midst of all the apparent conflict and stupidity in this world, you can still love. You can still have compassion. You can still reach out and say, "I'll help anyway." That's Spirit and God manifesting through you to the God in all people. It is a gift for both you and them. It's what this world is all about.

To reach the Mystical Traveler Consciousness, you must manifest living love. You must consistently give in living service. Love will not stay stagnant within one individual; it is always in a state of motion. It is the way God shares His nature with the world, and it "sleeps" if it is not shared.

Open yourself to serve Spirit. The opportunity to be of service may come on any level, including in areas you don't expect. Be open to the opportunities to serve, wherever and however they may appear. If you resist or serve from a place of resentment and irritation, it will come back on you. If you serve with loving concern and kindness, you will be rewarded more than you ever thought possible, and that reward may be the ability to do more.

When you move into a consciousness of service, you realize that the first thing you have to do is love. If you drop out of loving, you have also dropped out of service, and you may be doing things mechanically. You are no longer being of service; you are now being of "slaving," where you feel like you are a slave to something. When loving comes back in, then the serving reappears.

The negative attitude says, "Why are people always coming to me and loading me down with their troubles? Why do I attract them to me?" That attitude perceives life as a burden, and that is certainly one point of view. But other people say, "Thank God I can be of service. I am here to serve these people on whatever level and in whatever capacity I can." When we recognize our love of humanity, we do whatever has to be done to express that love to and with others.

Service is the highest form of consciousness in the physical world, and living love is the service of the moment. Living love is not fearful. It can reach out and touch and share without abusing or corrupting. It brings a blessing simply by its presence. So if you ever have the opportunity to help someone, do it. Those acts of kindness come back to you when you need them. Compassion is catching, and loving is contagious. We should have an epidemic!

And if you strive to have a pleasant disposition while you're doing whatever you're doing in the world, there is a greater tendency for your Soul, which is so perfect and so loving, to radiate out of your pleasant disposition. A truly pleasant disposition is loving, compassionate, and empathetic, with the ability to know what's going on in the world because it is not run by the ego. If you take that same pleasantness back inside you, you live with an abundance of enthusiasm that overflows to others. Now, that is truly helping the planet.

When you see the positive in all things, when you are of service to yourself and others, when you work always to lift yourself and others, you are living love.

THE LOVE OF THE SPIRITUAL HEART

This is the age of living love, and it manifests each time you enter into the love of the spiritual heart. The message of this age is that God's love is manifest here and now, within each person. When love is manifested and precipitated down, accepted and expressed, there is no more to be done.

When you bring yourself into a loving consciousness with all things and with the one consciousness that is everywhere, peace and harmony will enfold your heart and you will recognize within every level of your beingness that there is only love. We are continually awakening ourselves in other people's hearts and allowing them to awaken themselves in our hearts and thereby knowing more of

God consciousness. God's Spirit will function on love, on acceptance, on persistence, and on enthusiasm, joy, and elation.

When you, in your individual way, tune in to that which is divine love, where you know goodness dwells, the place where you truly live and express calmly, peacefully, and with love, then your behavior becomes a true representation of the Christ within you. When this process starts, you are opening the portals of your Soul. Awakening to the Soul is not an intellectual process; it is a state of being and doing.

Home is where the spirit of Christ reigns eternally, and that is within the loving heart. So awaken to the Christ, live in the Christ, live in your spiritual heart. When you love and are loving, you experience your heart and the heart of God. The larger your spiritual heart becomes and the more you live in the center of your spiritual heart, the more you'll discover that you are awake in the heart of all the world.

The positive level of the emotions is a joyful, blissful feeling. It's a good feeling towards all of God in all Its manifest forms throughout all creation, and it's the action of truly exemplifying the loving heart. God speaks to you through your heart. God brings peace to your life. You can know happiness, and you can know love. There is nothing else worth knowing.

When you look to the spiritual heart for your fulfillment, when you become pure of heart, when you let the spiritual heart speak, when you love—then the body, mind, and emotions follow, and you express total loving.

The heart knows the truth, and it is through the heart that we perceive Spirit. When the spiritual heart is open, then the spiritual eye is opened. Then love flows back and forth, and the Soul is awakened to its glory. You are in paradise even though you live in this physical world. The physical body will still express emotional and mental qualities, but your energies, your direction, and your upliftment come from the Soul. And that, Beloved, is a beautiful place to live.

Let your love be your guiding star. Let it be in your breath. Then you live in the heart of God. All things are made new, and God is personally present, all the time. When you express loving towards one another, this holds you more in the consciousness of grace, and in that consciousness of grace, all things are made new. Then each person resurrects to the consciousness of God and becomes the Beloved and walks with the consciousness of the Traveler right into the Heart of Hearts, right into God.

Baruch Bashan.

GLOSSARY

Baruch Bashan (bay-roosh' bay-shan'). Hebrew words meaning "the blessings already are." The blessings of Spirit exist in the here and now.

Beloved. The Soul, the God within.

Christ Consciousness. A universal consciousness of pure Spirit. Exists within each person through the Soul.

Holy Spirit. The positive energy of Light and Sound that comes from the Supreme God. The life force that sustains everything in all creation.

initiate. In MSIA, a person who has been connected to the Sound Current of God through initiation.

initiation tone. In MSIA, spiritually charged words (names of God) given to an initiate in a Sound Current initiation.

Inner Master. The inner expression of the Mystical Traveler, existing within a person's consciousness.

karma. The law of cause and effect: as you sow, so shall you reap. The responsibility of each person for his or her actions.

Light. The energy of Spirit that pervades all realms of existence.

MSIA (Movement of Spiritual Inner Awareness). An organization whose major focus is to bring people into an awareness of Soul Transcendence. John-Roger is the founder.

Mystical Traveler. Term often used to refer to the person who is physically anchoring the energy of the Mystical Traveler Consciousness on the planet. This consciousness also exists within each person.

Mystical Traveler Consciousness. An energy from the highest source of Light and Sound whose spiritual directive on Earth is awakening people to the awareness of the Soul. This consciousness exists within each person.

Soul. The extension of God individualized within each human being. The divine in each person, the indwelling Christ, the God within.

Soul Awareness Discourses. Booklets that students in MSIA read monthly as their personal spiritual study.

Soul consciousness. Awareness of oneself as divine.

Soul realm. The first level where the Soul is consciously aware of its true nature, its pure beingness, its oneness with God.

Soul Transcendence. The process of moving the consciousness into the Soul realm and beyond.

Sound Current. The audible energy that flows from God through all realms. The spiritual energy on which a person returns to the heart of God.

Spirit. The essence of creation. Infinite and eternal.

spiritual exercises. Chanting *Hu, Ani-Hu,* or one's initiation tone. An active technique of bypassing the mind and emotions by using a spiritual tone to connect to the Sound Current. *(Hu* is Sanskrit and is an ancient name of God, and *Ani* adds the quality of empathy.)

spiritual eye. The area in the center of the head, back from the center of the forehead. Used to see inwardly. Also called the third eye.

wheel of incarnation. The reincarnation, re-embodiment cycle.

FOR MORE INFORMATION FROM JOHN-ROGER

"Certainty of the Soul" *(Audiotape #2552)*. A sweet seminar about the Traveler's work in showing us the Lord that dwells in each of us.

"The Power of Love" *(Audiotape #2075)*. The divine love is inside of you.

"Impressions of the Soul" *(Audiotape #2060)*. A lovely seminar on how to find the Soul.

"The Divine Communion" *(Audiotape #3212)*. A beautiful seminar about knowing God, partaking of the divine communion, and knowing the joy of Spirit.

"How to Find Happiness" *(Audiotape #1108)*. Looking for happiness "out there" brings sorrow. Finding happiness through the God within brings joy.

Walking with the Lord (Paperbound book #930-0). A useful book of inspiration and information on spiritual exercises.

Living in Grace (Audiotape packet #3903; CD packet #3903-CD). Six tapes or CDs on the themes of forgiveness, grace, and peace.

"The Sound Current: The Road Home" *(Audiotape #7493; English with French translation)*. An excellent overview of MSIA and initiation.

"Communication in a Safe Place" *(Audiotape #7536)*. Keys to clear and loving communication.

"Finding the Hidden One Through a Balanced Body" *(Audiotape #2109)*. Techniques to bring the physical body into balance to find the Divine within you.

SOUL AWARENESS DISCOURSES

A Course in Soul Transcendence

Soul Awareness Discourses are designed to teach Soul Transcendence, which is becoming aware of yourself as a Soul and as one with God, not as a theory, but as a living reality. They are for people who want a consistent, time-proven approach to their spiritual unfoldment.

A set of Soul Awareness Discourses consists of 12 booklets, one to study and contemplate each month of the year. As you read each Discourse, you can activate an awareness of your Divine essence and deepen your relationship with God.

The Discourses are spiritual in nature, and many people find them compatible with their religious beliefs. In fact, most people find that Discourses support the experience of whatever path, philosophy, or religion (if any) they choose to follow. Simply put, Discourses are about eternal truths and the wisdom of the heart.

The first year of Discourses addresses topics ranging from creating success in the world to working hand-in-hand with Spirit.

A yearly set of Discourses is regularly $100. MSIA is offering the first year of Discourses at an introductory price of $50. Discourses come with a full, no-questions-asked, money-back guarantee. If at any time you decide this course of study is not right for you, simply return it, and you will promptly receive a full refund.

To order Discourses, contact the Movement of Spiritual Inner Awareness at 1-800-899-2665 or order@msia.org, or visit www.msia.org.

ABOUT THE AUTHOR

A teacher and lecturer of international stature, John-Roger is an inspiration in the lives of many people around the world. For over four decades, his wisdom, humor, common sense, and love have helped people to discover the Spirit within themselves and find health, peace, and prosperity.

With two co-authored books on the *New York Times* Bestseller List to his credit and more than three dozen self-help books and audio albums, John-Roger offers extraordinary insights on a wide range of topics.

He is the founder of the nondenominational Church of the Movement of Spiritual Inner Awareness (MSIA), which focuses on Soul Transcendence; founder and chancellor of the University of Santa Monica; founder and president of Peace Theological Seminary & College of Philosophy; founder of Insight Seminars and of the Institute for Individual and World Peace.

John-Roger has given over 6,000 lectures and seminars worldwide, many of which are televised nationally on his cable program, *That Which Is,* through the Network of Wisdoms. He has been a featured guest on *Larry King Live* and appears regularly on radio and television.

An educator and minister by profession, John-Roger continues to transform lives by educating people in the wisdom of the spiritual heart.

For more information about John-Roger, you may also visit: www.john-roger.org.

We welcome your comments and questions.

Mandeville Press
P.O. Box 513935
Los Angeles, California 90051-1935
323-737-4055
jrbooks@mandevillepress.org
www.mandevillepress.org

www.ingramcontent.com/pod-product-compliance
Lightning Source LLC
LaVergne TN
LVHW050941080826
845145LV00004B/1353